31 days to write better copy

A day to day approach to writing copy that sells

DENISE FAY

Logo & book cover designed by Pixelpool Design
Backcover photo by Cowley Photography

Foreword

Congratulations on making the smart move and purchasing the *'31 days to write better copy'* book. You now have a hard copy that you can refer to again and again.

The guys in the know say that we are bombarded with thousands of pieces of marketing literature every day. I think it's more than that to be honest with the amount of billboards, 30 second radio ads, Internet ads, emails, product placements in films and TV series that we are exposed to.

It's hard to get your message through to others and the first step is knowing how to write better. This book is broken into manageable steps so you can change or improve a skill a day...or sooner should you wish.

You've made the investment in terms of money so now you need to invest your time. Copywriting is the secret to good marketing. Time flies by so quickly and before you know it, you'll have bought the book but done little with it. I urge you to schedule time every day or every few days to read and practice each skill.

Chances are your competitors are not focusing on their copy. So you have the added advantage. Make the most of it.

Your customers and prospects need you – so start writing!

To your continued and even bigger success,

Denise

Table of Contents

Day 1 - Understanding What your Reader Wants to Read

The first task in the '*31 days to write better copy*' is to understand what your reader wants to read. Before you put pen to paper, fingers to keypad, you need to take a detailed look at who your reader is and what they like to read.

Identifying exactly who that person or segment is will make it easier for you to relate straight away. It makes talking to them so much easier. You use their language and you answer their needs.

Carpenters have a saying 'Measure twice and cut once.' That same logic can be applied to your written communication. Taking take time out to really analyze who your audience is for your particular piece of writing will give you two results:

1. You'll gain control over the writing, thus avoiding procrastination
2. You'll write a more effective piece, thus creating the relationship

It's easier said than done, analyzing what your audience wants. Seeing your message through your reader's eyes is really important. Here are three different anecdotes.

It's all about me, isn't it?

Take a look at these two pieces of information. They are both brief **'About Us'** pages. One was the original paragraph; the other we changed after analyzing the audience.

About us 1:

> We are an IT company based in Coolock. Serving North County Dublin, we have been in business for over 15 years. 100% Irish owned, we provide a high quality and cost effective IT outsource service.

About us 2:

> We sell, maintain and support IT equipment to businesses in the North County Dublin region. Businesses who do not have an internal IT support can rely on us 24 hours a day, 365 days a year to support their computers, networks and IT peripheries.

Based on these small snippets of information, which would make you pick up the phone?...(and yes, you have to pick one.)

The audience was small business owners and **About us2** got a better return. It said simply what ABC company can do for it's audience.

Lesson: The audience of small businesses didn't want jargon, they wanted to see the benefits.

Duh! Everyone knows what marketing is

Even copywriters get it wrong! When I first started my marketing consultancy in 2006, I produced a lovely three-fold flyer. The key message was that marketing can really benefit a business.

I quickly found out that the audience I was targeting (small businesses in a provincial town) equated marketing with advertising. They didn't see marketing as a process that included strategic planning, communication strategy, the Internet, networking and advertising. They simply saw marketing = advertising; they didn't need advertising and hence my cleverly worded letter was binned.

Lesson: Just because you know what you're talking about doesn't necessarily mean your audience does.

Say it as it is...for your audience

Tell your audience succinctly what it is they want to hear. In 1660, Blaise Pascal wrote in a post-script to a letter "*I made this letter longer than usual because I lack the time to make it shorter.*" (Provincial Letters XVI, 1660)

Nice excuse at the end after his audience suffered the excessive length.

Lesson: Avoid noise and get to the crux of what your audience wants to hear.

Action: Analyze a recent piece of literature

Take a piece of literature that you've recently produced or plan to produce. It could be a page on your website, a blog post or a sales email.

Look at it and ask yourself the following questions:
1. Who is this piece aimed at?
2. What is the reader's purpose for reading it?
3. How knowledgeable is your reader on the topic?
4. How interested are they in the topic?
5. Have you included the most relevant message to your reader?

Once you can see your message through your reader's eyes, you can establish a connection with them much easier.

Day 2 - What to Do if Words Don't Come Easy

Back in 1982, FR David sold 8 million copies of his song 'Words'. He sang:

"Words don't come easy to me,
how can I find the way to make you see I love you,
words don't come easy."

If like Mr David, words don't come easy to you, then this is the day for you. While you may not want to tell your new and existing customers that you love them, you do want them to know why they should work with you.

Understanding what your reader wants to read

The '*31 Days to Write Better Copy*' is not a sequential series. However, I wanted to devote Day 2 to follow up on the homework from Day 1. Day 1 of the '*31 Days to Write Better Copy*' helped you look at your message from your audience's point of view.

From Day 1's homework, you will have gotten a better understanding of

- Your reader's purpose for reading your piece

- The level of interest they have in your subject
- How knowledgeable they are on your topic

Fail to plan and plan to fail

One of the main reasons that words don't come easy to many people is because they don't feel confident enough. Most business owners and executives are confident speaking on the phone and one-on-one yet words fail when writing.

The more preparation you do before you write, the more effective the piece will be and the more confident you will be when writing.

Write a list

Once you've found out more about your target audience, you should create a list of what they like, what they don't like, what language they use and how formal (or not) their interactions are. This will give you greater awareness of your audience. You'll discover things such as:

- Your audience likes to answer questions
- They prefer straight-talking information
- Your readers like testimonials
- Your audience thinks white-papers are unnecessary
- They wouldn't read a blog if you paid them

A secondary benefit to writing a list is that you'll now start noticing what other suppliers are doing or saying, what they are advertising and how they write their messages. Be prepared to be inspired for future promotional material.

Where to look for information

Many clients ask where they can find out more about their audience. You won't find it in any one specific place. But reading a few places will allow you to join the dots and you'll start to see a common theme.

Forums

These can be hidden gems when looking for information. People who comment on forums generally do so in an informal nature. There are forums on everything, from general interest to business; entertainment to farming. You just need to pick the right ones for you.

A good starting point is Big Boards which promotes itself as the largest list of message boards and forums on the web http://www.big-boards.com/. Another way is to Google a local forum related to your business.

Trade Magazines

Nothing beats reading about your industry than trade magazines. You can read the tone in which articles are written, giving you a good indication of the tone and style that readers like. It will also give you ideas as to what is topical or of interest to your audience.

Newspapers

While more general in nature, you can pick out stories that you know your audience is interested in. When reading stories applicable to your audience, ask yourself what is the headline, what is the first paragraph and what is quoted. Such answers will offer more information about your audience.

Social Media

The Internet is alive with social media sites, such as Facebook, Twitter, Linkedin, MySpace, Audioboo, blogs, YouTube - the list is endless. Find your 'water cooler' sites. By this I mean, where your audience hangs out and has the chat, like the watercooler at work. You'll find much information about your readers likes and dislikes here.

A word of caution, however, be careful to validate opinions. Make sure that they are not the opinion of one or two in your industry. If you write to the strong opinions of one or two and not the majority, it could be detrimental.

Action: Find out what your reader reads

1. Take an hour to browse through the Internet, trade publications and the newspapers that you have to hand.
2. Bookmark sites that you think are worth monitoring
3. Tear out articles of interest and put them into a folder called 'Writing Ideas'

Becoming aware of what your reader wants to read will give you the confidence to write. You'll soon find that words will come easier to you, as will ideas.

As a reward for doing your homework, here is the link to FR David's romantic ballad - http://www.youtube.com/watch?v=Ob6hM6f9U4s

Day 3 - Why Two Advil Won't Resolve Writer's Block

Many people encounter writer's block. It's almost like a sickness. You sit at the computer to write but nothing happens. But unlike other sicknesses, you can't take a few painkillers and make it go away.

The Hollywood effect

Don't you love Hollywood? You watch a film and agonize with the main character who is almost torn apart because he can't write. Then he up-sticks and moves to an idyllic location, far removed from reality. Inspired by the sea view or the movement of the trees in the forest, the writer begins to write and all is well with the world.

Well guess what? You live in the real world and you more than likely can't jet off to the South of France whenever you've a website to write or a customer ezine. You need a prescription to your writer's block that doesn't involve scenic views!

Throw away your excuses

Someone once said to me, the worst thing about traveling is the traveling. However, the worst thing about writing isn't writing, it's getting started. If I had a euro for everytime I heard an excuse, I'd be a very wealthy woman.

Here are some excuses that I've encountered. If there are one or two that you can relate to, I've written you a prescription to get over your sickness.

Condition No. 1: Procrastination

You want to write and you sit down to write. However, you decide that a coffee will help the creative process so you head to the coffee maker. While making your coffee, you realise that the coffee-pot really needs a good clean. You'll do it now because it won't take long. Two hours, a few phone calls later and it's time to meet a client. You'll do the website later.

Prescription

1. Let go of the guilt. Understand that procrastination is natural. It really is. Everyone does it. Even the top gurus in your field do it. It takes time to warm up to a topic.

2. When you're using a particular task to avoid writing (e.g. cleaning the coffee pot), allow your subconscious to think about your subject. Have a little chat to yourself.

3. Give yourself a strict deadline. The article or website needs to be written by X day.

Condition No. 2: Not knowing what to write

Fail to plan and plan to fail. We discussed this in Day 1 and Day 2 of the '*31 Days to Write Better Copy*' book. If you don't know your audience, or what they want to read, then it's so hard to sit down and write.

Prescription

1. Do research to understand what your customers want to read.
2. Find out as much information as you can.
3. When you see an idea for an article, write it down straight-away on your phone, a piece of paper, a notebook. Inspiration comes when you're least expecting it.

Condition No. 3: Fear of failure

When you write, do you think that you put yourself out there to be judged and criticized? Has previous experience shown you that people will argue over your choice of wording, let alone choice of concept?

If so, don't worry – you're not alone. I had a conversation recently with a client and we discussed at length about the words '*slim*' or '*svelte*'. The client wanted '*svelte*' because it sounded more "*sophisticated*". We went with '*svelte*' in the end.

Don't let this stop you from writing. If people argue with you, then it shows passion for your work so take it as a compliment. Seriously.

Prescription

1. Learn to appreciate that people will criticize your copy.
2. Research your audience. This will help you write confidently.
3. Remember the 80/20 rule. 80% of the people will relate to your copy, 20% will take it apart. And that's totally fine.

Condition No. 4: Don't know where to start

Sometimes people feel overwhelmed about where to start. Do you often find yourself talking to yourself and asking whether you should write the heading first and follow a sequential process? Or should I write features and benefits and build from there? If you're constantly asking questions, you tend not to write.

Prescription

1. Learn to love editing. Writing the first draft is just that - the first draft. The key to successful writing is editing.
2. Just write. Start anywhere.
3. Get yourself a writing system and follow it.

On a final note, recognize that writing good copy is hard work. The hard part is getting started. Take the prescriptions I've offered - they are the writers equivalent to two paracetamol. Then start writing.

Action: Ask yourself some honest questions

Ask yourself honestly

1. What stops you from writing?
2. What stops you from writing well?
3. Draw your own list and give yourself your own prescription.
4. Follow my prescription for your particular condition.

Day 4 - How to Write Killer Headlines - The Basics

A headline can make or break a sales letter, website page, newsletter, email, email newsletter, blog post or twitter post. In fact, everything you write should have a killer headline.

Headlines are the gatekeeper of an article or ad. If it's good, people will read on. If it isn't, then your email or sales letter hits the recycling bin or gets the delete button treatment.

Just as the purpose of the first sale is to get a second sale, the purpose of the first sentence is to get your reader to read the second sentence and so forth.

The first sentence doesn't start in the body of the text. It starts with the headline.

Still need convincing?

If you're still not sure about the importance of headlines, check out these snippets from the experts:

According to David Ogilvy, founder of the Ogilvy & Mather advertising agency and author of Confessions of an Advertising Man:

"On the average, 5 times as many people read the headlines as read the body copy. It follows that unless your headline sells your product, you have wasted 90% of your money."

Google: *"Recent research suggests that users decide to stay or leave your site in 8 seconds or less -- in that short amount of time, headlines are the one piece of copy that users will actually read."*

There are a number of basics that you need to get right when writing headlines.

1. Identify who your audience is

Your headline should change depending on whether or not your audience is freezing, cold or warm. By this I mean, will your audience be reading your article/letter/ad for the first time? Will they know who you are, will they know your product name?

You can tailor headlines to suit your audience's knowledge of you and your product. This will lead to more people reading your articles. Decide whether you are writing to sell or writing to engage.

2. Write for people first

You will read many articles extolling the virtues of headlines and keywords for Search Engine Optimization (SEO). SEO helps raise your profile on the search engines. Some exponents argue that writing for SEO is different than writing for reading's sake. My experience has shown that writing for people first will help with both SEO and click-through.

If you write as if you're talking to the person, chances are you're going to write a killer heading....and copy.

3. Ask yourself 'What's in it for me?'

If you want to lure people into your copy, then you need to ask yourself the question through the reader's eyes - "what's in it for me?". If you can't answer this, then you need to start again. No matter what way you structure your headline, it has to answer that important question.

4. Keep it short

The average or ideal length for a headline is five words. Shorter headlines give a better punch or a better sizzle to your message. If you are battling with more words, then simply make a sub-heading out of them or make use of punctuation.

5. Make it real

Under no circumstance should you write the best headline ever, but not have the copy to back it up. Or worse still, the product or service doesn't match up with the headline's benefits. Your headline has to support the copy just as the copy supports the headline.

The best headline in the world won't stop a bad story from ruining your reputation.

6. Keep it simple

I've seen numerous witty and clever headlines. Some work, a lot don't. My advice is to keep it simple. Don't be clever for clever's sake.

7. Start over

Once you've written your headline, ask yourself if you're happy with it. If you are, start over again. If you're not, start over again. You should spend as much time on your headline as you do on your copy. Do not stop until you are proud of your headline.

Action: 7 questions to ask yourself about your latest headline

Today, I'm relying on 7 questions which Clayton Makepeace*, one of the world's acclaimed copy-writers asked on a teleconference sometime ago.

Take a recent headline and ask yourself:

1. Does your headline touch a nerve?

2. Does it make a unique claim or statement?

3. Does it provoke curiosity?

4. Is it credible?

5. It is specific?

6. Does it have a news element?

7. Does it offer a compelling benefit for reading?

*Source: Clayton Makepeace teleconference, 12/20/06. (Courtesy of The Blog Squad)

Day 5 - How to Write Killer Headlines - 4 Techniques

Writing the headline can often cause the best copy-writer a panic attack. It is the gatekeeper of your article and will make the difference between whether it's read or not, never mind the sale. However, fear not, there are several techniques that you can use when creating your killer headline.

Remember when writing a headline, it should:

- Lull the reader into further reading
- Be emphatic
- Resonate with the reader
- Be persuasive

Don't forget to check out Day 4 - How to Write Killer Headlines - The Basics before using the following techniques.

Timeless Headlines

Coco Chanel once said "*Fashion fades, only style remains the same*". Applying that same logic to headlines, you could say "*Great stories are interesting, great headlines are timeless.*"

1. Ask a question

Forget about headlines for the moment. If you ask someone - your mum, your boss, a stranger - a question, what do they do? Answer it! Human nature wants to answer a question, rather than leave it hanging.

Asking a question in a headline leads the reader to read your copy - they feel compelled to answer the question. Depending on the product or service you're selling, be careful of closed questions. (Don't ask questions that require a yes or no answer.) You don't want to eliminate a substantial portion of your readership.

An emphatic question works well as does a question that impacts on a need.

There are a few headlines to swipe:

- What would an extra €5,000 a month mean to you?

- Fancy a cup-cake without the guilt?

- Who clse wants a celebrity figure?

- Want 31 ways to write better copy?

2. The 'Reason Why' headline

The 'Reason Why' is a very popular headline technique. It draws the reader in by giving them a reason to read the list.

With this type of headline, you typically write the copy first and then build the headline around it. Your copy will have a numbered list of features, tips or advice and then you incorporate it into your headline. This technique is a good one for creating credibility as the writer has taken time to write the list.

Examples in this technique include:

- 7 ways to....

- 3 reasons why....

- A - Z of Weight Loss

- A GREAT example - 31 Days to Write Better Copy.

3. The 'How to' Headline

The 'How to' Headline is a great one. If you can't come up with another headline, then use the 'How to' headline. You really can't go wrong. An adaptation of the 'How to' headline is 'How I...', 'How he...', 'How you...'

Some swipe headlines for your inspiration:

- How to write headlines that work

- How to make a better mousetrap

- How I made a fortune

4. Create curiosity

Curiosity killed the cat. It's the name of a band and a very well known proverb. It warns against being too curious. But again, human nature is a curious one. You see it with babies, they explore everything and everywhere. Newspaper shelves are filled with gossip and celebrity magazines because we are a curious breed.

You can create curiosity by making an outrageous statement, using word play, alliteration or taking off a well-known phrase.

- Want a Wonderful Warm Way to Welcome Winter?

- Advertising pays - but to whom?

- The most expensive lesson you'll ever learn

- What if this happened on your wedding day

- Life is like a box of chocolate covered strawberries

Action: Go headline hunting

Today, I want you to go headline hunting.

Go through your RSS feed, your emails, the newspaper, the website, Twitter, Facebook, whatever you read today and pick your favorite headline of the day.

Explain why you thought so. You don't need to share it with me or anyone else – but if you want to feel free. This task is to make you aware of the headlines that are out there – some good, some bad but like aliens (apparently!), they're all around.

Day 6 - Another 4 Ways to Write Headlines that Work

Today I'm continuing with the topic of headlines. I want you to know the basics and have 8 techniques in your copywriting arsenal to write killer headlines.

To recap, the basics, from Day 4 - How to Write Killer Headlines - The Basics, are:

- Identify Who Your Audience Is
- Write for People First
- Ask yourself 'What's in it for me?'
- Keep it Short
- Make it Real
- Keep it Simple
- Start Over

The objective of a headline is to:

- Lull the reader into further reading
- Be emphatic
- Resonate with the reader
- Be persuasive

Here are another four ways to make your headlines timeless.

1. The 'News' headline

What can I say about the news headline? It's a headline that describes a news-worthy story. It's obviously the most used headline, because people want to tell news and people want to read news.

When writing a news headline, please make sure it's compelling. Just because it's news-worthy to you, doesn't mean that it's newsworthy to the reader and a journalist (if you're pitching to a paper).

If you're writing news headlines, learn from the people who do it every day. Go to your library, look at all the newspapers they have and read the different headlines for the same story. It is an interesting way to learn to write news headlines.

2. The 'Command' headline

This headline always reminds me of Nike's *'Just do it'*. It's snappy, to the point and has a strong action in it. This headline tells the reader what he or she needs to do. There is no doubt about it. Start with a strong verb.

Take a look at these command headlines:

- Discover the fortune that lies hidden in your business

- Throw away your calculator

- Use a lawyer to your detriment

- Dare to be famous

3. The 'Testimonial' headline

The testimonial headline uses a customer testimonial as a headline. It works well for websites, ad copy (online and offline) and sales letters. It gives your reader external proof that your product or service offers value and works. The testimonial headline is a departure from the typical five-worded headline.

Use a testimonial which your customer has written. Make sure you use quotation marks so your reader knows that it is a testimonial.

These are a few testimonial headlines:

"I used the headline articles from the '31 Days to Write Better Copy' to re-write a headline on a sales page. We doubled our sales and actually ran out of stock."

"By attending your workshop, I now have a clearer understanding of

researching my audience. I've just realized I've been targeting the wrong people but I'm going to change that. Today!"

4. The 'Direct' headline

The last technique I'm sharing today is the direct one. Say it as it is. You don't use any clever headlines, no questions, no lists, no emotion. It just tells you what the story is about.

Here are some examples:

- Free webinar on Linkedin

- Become a waitress in a Michelin-starred restaurant

- Sale on Washing Machines Starts Today

- 2 for 1 on every bottle of wine

Action: Go headline hunting

Like yesterday, I want you to go headline hunting.

Go through your RSS feed, your emails, the newspaper, Twitter, Facebook, whatever you read today and pick your favorite headline of the day. Explain why you thought so.

By now, you have 8 key headline techniques in your copywriting arsenal. Test them and see what works for your audience.

Day 7 - The Science of Paragraph Writing

A paragraph is a group of sentences that develop an idea. It can also be part of an extended idea. A document is made up of several paragraphs. Mastering the art of paragraph writing will make writing easier and more effective.

There are a few steps to writing a successful paragraph. Often when you begin writing, ideas start to flow. This is great for creativity purposes but in order for a paragraph to make sense to the reader, it should be focused. By all means write the ideas down as they come but when editing the paragraph, follow these three steps.

Three Steps to Successful Paragraphs

1. Decide on the topic sentence

Paragraph development begins with planning. Once you have decided the objective of your document, you should break it down into chunks.

These 'chunks' or paragraphs need their own focus. Enter the topic sentence. The topic sentence defines what can be included (or not) in the paragraph. It is generally one sentence and is placed at the beginning of the paragraph. In essence, it tells your reader what the paragraph will be about. It will also help you to avoid 'noise' - writing irrelevant details which distract the reader from the main point.

I've seen writers who begin every paragraph with a topic sentence. To emphasize the point, they bold the text. Immediately the reader gets the point and then decides to read further.

2. Back up with support

Substantiating your idea or topic with facts or explanations is often overlooked but very important for a number of reasons:

a) It supports the point you are making.

b) It creates further interest in your paragraph (and document).

c) It helps you write a concluding statement.

d) It can lead the reader to the next paragraph.

3. Write a concluding statement

With every good story, there is a beginning, a middle and an end. Your paragraph should finish with a concluding statement. A concluding statement can have three aims:

a) It summarizes the points you made within the paragraph.

b) It ties up any loose ends made within the paragraph.

c) It can lead the reader into the next paragraph by introducing the topic in the next paragraph.

Action: Analyze your recent document for paragraph science

Careful planning before writing makes your document flow. What I want you to do for homework today is to:

1. Click onto your website home page (or latest blog post)
2. Look at the first three paragraphs

Then ask yourself:

3. Does it have a topic sentence?
4. What are you trying to say?
5. Does it compel the reader to read more?
6. Does it have a concluding statement?

If not, then you should apply this three step process to your home page copy and change around the text.

Day 8 - The Art of Paragraph Writing

Yesterday, I wrote about the science of paragraph writing. Today, I'm talking about the art of paragraph writing. If you have a paragraph that looks good, there is a better chance that it will be read. Think about it. How many times have you looked at a document and groaned? The A4 page is one long paragraph.

You look at the document and groan again. Where do you start? What's the point of it? You start reading and by the third sentence, you're bored. You skip to the last line and hope that it has a nice concluding statement.

I had a friend at college who rarely put paragraphs into their text. Comparing his document with mine, there was a stark difference. Using his style, the **'Three Steps to Successful Paragraphs'** would look very different to mine (pages 31 & 32)

Three Steps to Successful Paragraphs

1. Decide on the topic sentence

Paragraph development begins with planning. Once you have decided the objective of your document, you should break it down into chunks. These 'chunks' or paragraphs need their own focus. Enter the topic sentence. The topic sentence defines what can be included (or not) in the paragraph. It is generally one sentence and is placed at the beginning of the paragraph. In essence, it tells your reader what the paragraph will be about. It will also help you to avoid 'noise' - writing irrelevant details which distract the reader from the main point. I've seen writers who begin every paragraph with a topic sentence. To emphasize the point, they bold the text. Immediately the reader gets the point and then decides to read further.

2. Back up with support

Substantiating your idea or topic with facts or explanations is often overlooked but very important for a number of reasons. It supports the point you are making, it creates further interest in your paragraph (and document), it helps you write a concluding statement and it can lead the reader to the next paragraph.

3. Write a concluding statement

With every good story, there is a beginning, a middle and an end. Your paragraph should finish with a concluding statement. A concluding statement can have three aims: It summarizes the points you made within the paragraph, it ties up any loose ends made within the paragraph and it can lead the reader into the next paragraph by introducing the topic in the next paragraph.

Give your paragraphs a chance to be read. The above is quite intimidating; with little white space, it's hard to take a breath. You're reading it but there are no automatic breaks. Even us Irish take a deep breath in when we're having a conversation!

Here are three ways to help you along the way.

1. Length of your paragraphs

How long should a paragraph be is an age old question. To truly answer it, I would recommend that a paragraph be as long as it takes to write, explain and conclude one idea.

However, reading style has changed. We prefer to read and glance rather than sit down and read long copy. Short paragraphs are read quicker than long ones.

There is no real rule of thumb as it's important to make your point in your paragraph. However, in my experience, it should be no more than 7 lines. If a paragraph is more than 12 lines, then you should break it up into two or three paragraphs.

Don't worry if you tend to write long paragraphs. You can easily edit them from here on in. If you write long paragraphs, look at the points you make. Where there is a logical point or a leading statement, then that would be place to cut the long paragraph and start a new one.

2. Design of your paragraphs

The length of your document not only allows for easy reading of your document, it also adds variety to it. You know when you're at a conference and the speaker talks in the same monotone, well, keeping your paragraphs all the same size can be just as drowsy. You want to add a bit of rhythm to your document. Changing the length adds that bit of salsa to your documents. Also, have a paragraph of one sentence or two lines right beside a longer paragraph. It highlights the two points in the two paragraphs.

Use indentation as another means of designing your paragraph. Some articles or letters indent the first line of the paragraph (like this one).

Another way to add a splash of paragraph design is to emphasize the first letter of the paragraph. How many times have you seen this in a children's book? It's eye-catching and adds a bit of depth to your story. It's primarily used at the beginning of the document.

3. Include everyone's favorite word

One of the last ways to add a bit of art to your paragraphs is to add the word '*you*', '*your*' or '*yours*'.

What is anyone's favorite topic?

Themselves! Write your paragraph as if you're talking to the person. Saying '*you*' or a variation of '*you*', the reader can see themselves in the text and can relate straight-away.

Action: Analyze your webcopy for paragraph art

Take a look at your web copy. Can you:

1. Change the length of your paragraphs to add depth to your page?

2. Use a design element to lift the words off the page?

3. Add more use of the word 'you' to your text to relate to your reader?

Day 9 - How to Write a Successful Bulleted List

Because of our style of glance-reading, bulleted lists are very popular. They help emphasize a point and allow the reader to take information in quickly. However, they are often over-used and incongruent. This article provides three pieces of advice when writing successful bullets.

Just look at this example and it's clear why bullets work.

The '***Reason Why***' is a very popular headline technique. It draws the reader in by giving them a reason to read the list. Examples in this technique include: • 7 ways to.... • 3 reasons why.... • A - Z of Weight Loss • 31 Days to Write Better Copy.	The '***Reason Why***' is a very popular headline technique. It draws the reader in by giving them a reason to read the list. Examples in this technique include 7 ways to..., 3 reasons why...., A-Z of Weight Loss and 31 Days to Write Better Copy.

In the first example, straightaway you can see four ways to write

'*Reason Why*' headlines.

In the second example, it's harder to find the examples. Bullets serve a really useful purpose in documents.

Bulleted lists add a dimension to copywriting that can't be done any other way. It follows numbering in it's ability to state clearly a thought or support an idea. For that reason, they should be used sparingly. Overuse them and they lose their importance. If your document requires many sets of bullet lists, then you should reconsider the text.

Here are three things to consider when crafting your bullets or bulleted list.

1. Parallelism in bullets

There are two parallelisms that should be considered when writing bulleted lists: conceptual parallelism and grammatical parallelism.

A. Conceptual parallelism

Conceptual parallelism occurs where the bullets support the sentence made just previous to the bulleted list. The points made in the bullets should not overlap and should be specific to the point being made.

For example, a Finishing School in Dublin (www.thefinishingschool.ie)

produced a flyer promoting their courses for the year. It included all the topics that the course covers.

This list is conceptually parallel:

Course Topics Include:
- How to get the most out of your make-up
- Increase your efficiency at home to save time & money
- How to behave at parties to maximize your fun
- Know how much to give (and get) as a tip
- How to enter a group conversation

Each topic starts with a strong verb and describes the courses that the Finishing School will teach.

This list is not conceptually parallel:

Reasons for the weight-gain included:
- Bad diet
- Lack of exercise
- Inability to read weigh scales because of lost glasses

The last point isn't a reason for weigh-gain. It's not specific to the point. It could be a lead-in to the paragraph after the bulleted list.

B. Grammatical parallelism

Every bullet of a list should have the same grammatical structure. If you begin a bullet with an active verb, then each bullet should begin with an active verb. Similarly, if you begin with an noun, then continue on with a noun.

This is a grammatically correct list:

At school, little Luke does a number of tasks. Luke does the following:

- Washes the dishes with the teacher
- Runs around the playground
- Draws colored pictures
- Tells a story about his weekend activities

Each bullet starts with a verb and describes what Luke does.

This is an incorrect grammatical list:

Each teacher deems what is important to her class. This can include:

- Washing dishes with the children
- Provide coloring pencils for art work
- Fill up the sandpit when empty

This list begins with an active verb, (-ing), and follows with two verbs.

If all words ended with -ing, then it would be grammatically correct.

2. Punctuation of bullets

Everyone has their own idea of punctuation of bullets. When I wrote the word processing module for '***Training for ECDL, A Practical course in StarOffice 8***', we had many discussions over the punctuation of bullets. Do we put a comma after each one, do we put a full stop or do we just leave them blank?

Let me tell it to you straight - **there is no one real and fast rule of punctuation of bullets**. Some teachers or writers put a full-stop at the end of each bullet as it represents it's own point. Others say that every bulleted point leads to the last bullet and therefore only the last bullet has a full stop. Others say semi-colons should be used.

Take my advice: Create your own style guidelines. That way, every piece of literature you produce will be consistent.

3. Number of bullets

Have you ever seen a list that seems to just go and on and you can't remember any details from it?

Not only does a long list defeat the purpose of scan-ability, it also lends itself to not being read or remembered. George Miller back in the 1950s put forward a theory that the short term memory can process 7 (plus or minus 2) pieces of information.

This means that anymore than 7 items in a bullet and the short-term memory may not process it. To get the best use of your bulleted list, make sure you have no more than seven items.

You can take this one step further and only have 5-7 words per bullet.

Action: Create your own style

Look at how your organization typically writes list of bullets and see if there is any consistency. Do you:

- use commas at the end of a sentence,
- use periods or full stops at the end.
- have no punctuation at the end
- have a mixture of punctuation

Decide on a style and use it from here on in. Just be consistent with your bulleted lists.

Day 10 - Getting to Grips with Sentence Structure

At the heart of everything you write is a sentence. Yet it often gets neglected when a person sits down to write. It's normally taken for granted. Taking care of your sentences can make a huge difference to your reader. It can entertain them or if done badly, can bore and confuse them.

1. The basics

copywriting is very different to academic writing. The aim of copywriting is to make sure your promotional copy is engaging and readable to the **audience**. It doesn't follow pure grammatical rules.

However, the one grammatical rule it should follow is the rule of word order. Sentences should follow the normal sequence of **subject-verb-object**.

Take a look at these two sentences:

The program, 31 days to write better copy, continues to be widely read on a daily basis.

Continuing to be well received is the program, 31 days to write better copy, by an increasing audience.

Which one reads better?

Sentence 1 reads well. You can understand it. It has a subject (the program), a verb (continues) and object (widely read).

Sentence 2, on the other hand, is cumbersome. The verb (continues) precedes the subject (the program) and object (audience).

When crafting sentences, think of your reader. You are taking up their time, whereby they could be doing something else. Appreciate that time by making your documents as readable and approachable as possible.

2. Sentence length

Adding variety to your sentences will add rhythm to your document and help to avoid it becoming boring. There is nothing worse than too many short sentences or too many long sentences.

This is a memo written by the head of garden depot for a large retail store:

We balanced the books this past summer when we noticed that tree manure sales were down by as much as turnover for grass seed went up. Chatting to the lads over at Westbere and they said that heavy rains kept people from gardening. In the end, we are up on sales by 25%.

This is how his assistant changed it before the memo went to the Board of Directors:

This summer, we made an overall profit of 25%. This is down on last year due to a number of reasons. Firstly, sales of tree manure, a high margin product, were down. Secondly, grass seed sales were the number one seller but have a very low margin. Thirdly, the unseasonal amount of rain discouraged people from regular gardening.

The first paragraph had a mixture of short and long sentences. The shortest sentence was 7 words; the longest 26. The second paragraph also had a mixture of short and long sentences. The shortest sentence was 9 words; the longest 15.

So both added variety to the sentence structure. However, as a group of sentences, the first paragraph has a lot of compressed information with no real specifics except for the last sentence. The reader will invariably have to read it again. Whereas with the second paragraph, the sentences flow well together.

The key to rhythmic sentences is to read aloud. You'll get a better feel for the sentence length and structure. You'll also sense if there is rhythm in the sentence or if it is mono-toned.

3. The (over) use of 'and'

'*And*' is a useful word. It joins two related thoughts of equal importance together. Too often it is over-used when two ideas are not of equal importance or when another word would suffice instead.

Here is a great example of using '*and*' correctly in a sentence:
"*The CFO is on holidays and the CEO is at a conference.*"

Here is an example where '*and*' is used incorrectly:
"*The CFO is on holidays and sales have decreased.*"

It implies that profits are down because the CFO is on holidays, when it is a mere coincidence. These two ideas or thoughts are not related.

Another way to write the above sentence is "*While the CFO is on holidays, sales have decreased.*" or "*Sales have decreased in the same time period that the CFO was away.*"

Try to reduce your use of the word '*and*'. Highlight every '*and*' that you have in your document and see if you can use another word. Here are three examples where '*and*' is used but another word or phrase could have been used.

Example 1:

Deliveries were delayed and orders were lost.

Because of the delay with deliveries, the company lost orders.

Example 2:

Appreciate your staff and your staff will be happy.

If you appreciate your staff, they will be happy

Example 3:

I arrived in Dublin and realized I'd forgotten the phone.

When I arrived in Dublin, I realized I'd forgotten the phone.

4. Link words

Sentences should roll together to keep with the flow of the document. If one sentence 'jars' after another one, the reader has to stop. This can lead to the meaning being lost, or the document being discarded.

Link sentences together using the following words. Begin a sentence with these where appropriate and the flow of your sentences should remain intact.

- Like
- Therefore
- So
- However
- Despite
- Notwithstanding
- Because

Action: Re-assess your 'about us' webpage

Take the 'About us' page from your website and re-assess it using the following questions

1. How many paragraphs do you have?
2. What's the longest sentence?
3. Can you break up the longest sentence into two shorter sentences?
4. How many '*and*'s' do you have (don't forget to highlight them)?
5. Do you use link words to connect sentences?

Edit the text after answering the questions.

Day 11 - The Rough Guide to Punctuation

Punctuation is a great way to clarify your message and add a voice to it. It breaks up your text into understandable sections and allows your document to flow.

If you were giving a speech or indeed having a conversation with someone, there is a natural time to take a break, pause, allow the information to sink in or the other person to speak up.

Punctuation allows you to do that in a document. Your speech pattern, your tone of voice, those quirky inflections that you have should all appear in a piece of text that you write.

The more I read about punctuation, the more I realize that punctuation is individual. Some writers will put a comma before '*and*' when talking about a series. (The box contained pens, pencils, and coloring pens) others will not use a comma before '*and*' (The box contained pens, pencils and coloring pens). Me personally, I don't use the comma before '*and*' as '*and*' lends itself to a pause.

There are rules, however, that apply and I've included the most popular ones here. Go through the list and find ways to use them more often. Perhaps, use a semi-colon instead of a full stop and two sentences. Try to break up your text by using all of them, not just a fullstop.

Remember the purpose of punctuation is to assist your reader understand your message. If you're trying to sell to them, mirror your tone or style as much as possible.

Punctuation marks & their explanation

The below shows the most popular punctuation marks and explains how you can use them in your copy or documents.

Mark	Name	General Use
.	Period or full stop	Signifies the end of a sentence and denotes an abbreviation. (e.g.) *Mr. Hennessy concluded the meeting at 6.04pm*
,	Comma	Indicates a pause in a sentence and separates the main clauses in a sentence. (e.g.) *The meeting began at 4pm with 5 members of staff, however two members arrived later.*
-	Dash	Adds another idea to a sentence - can be used instead of parenthesis. (e.g.) *The CFO gave his report after the CEO - outlining his proposal for change.*
:	Colon	Introduces examples, a bulleted list, a

		numbering list or a quotation. (e.g.) *The Marketing Director quoted the regional manager: "The campaign went really well."*
;	Semi-colon	Introduces a break in the sentence without using comma or fullstop. Also links two sentences together. (e.g.) *We would love to give a bonus; it's just so hard with no extra cash in the bank.*
( )	Parenthesis (or brackets)	Highlights an aside or an interruption. (e.g.) *We would love to give a bonus; it's just so hard with no extra cash in the bank (but the management team will receive a bonus).*
!	Exclamation point	Adds a bit of drama or excitement to a document. Rarely used in formal documents but frequently in adverts. (e.g.) *Stop! This might be the best offer you'll see all day.*
?	Question mark	Placed at the end of a direct question. (e.g.) *Did you place an order?* It is not used when asking an indirect question (e.g.) *I asked you if you had placed an order;* or when an informal inquiry is made over email (e.g.) *Can you let me know when you placed the order, Kind Regards....*

Action: Count your punctuation marks

Look at the services page of your website or a brochure that you're writing.

Highlight every punctuation mark that you have in the piece of text.

Can you change it or keep it?

Day 12 - Use Literary Devices to Make your Copy Engaging

There are a number of literary devices that you have to hand to make your copy more engaging. Writing is an art form; just as artists have their oils and brushes, writers have their own tools.

When I was in school, I loved using literary devices to liven up copy. I use them all the time when writing advertising copy. It helps the reader to really understand, to use their imagination to see what you are selling, not just your text.

Here are six literary techniques that you can use when writing your next copy-piece.

1. Alliteration

A sentence where the same letter is used at the beginning of each word in a sentence.

- *A Wonderful Warm Way to Welcome Winter*
- *31 ways to write words that win*

2. Hyperbole

The use of exaggeration to emphasize a point.

- *I told you a million times*
- *You're the biggest exaggerator in the world*

3. Metaphor

A phrase which compares one thing to another, that would otherwise not be similar. You need to use 'is' with a metaphor.

- *He is such a featherhead*
- *She is like a mule*

4. Metonym

A word or name of one thing is applied to something with which it is closely associated or is an attribute of thing itself.

- *"Tivo" or "Skyplus"* for recording a program
- *"The Crown"* for royalty
- *"The Hill"* for Ireland's Bellewstown Races (as the racecourse is on a hill)
- *"The Old Bill"* for the police

5. Oxymoron

A phrase where two contradictory terms are used for emphasis.

- *Clearly confused*
- *Pretty ugly*

6. Simile

A phrase that likens one thing with another that is not normally associated. You need to use 'as' or 'like' with a simile.

- *The box was as big as a house*
- *His copy was as dull as dishwater*
- *Her article read like a damp squid*
- *She's as stubborn as a mule*
- *As welcome as wasps on a sunny day*

Action: Practice writing literary devices

Think about the above 6 literary devices and write examples of them that come to mind. Don't think about your website or promotional material. Just think of examples, this will help you get used to writing and thinking about them.

You hear people say or write these literary devices. The trick is to tune into them. So use this space to write examples.

Day 13 - Use Sub-headings to Break up Your Text

Sub-headings serve an important purpose. They allow readers to skim an article and get an overall impression for the information within the document.

You can use sub-headings to break up long blocks of copy and highlight the document's important points. They can be tricky to get right but when you have them right, they can be golden.

Lets get down to basics. There are other ways to break up text in a document, some which we've discussed already in this '*31 days to write better copy*' book. So why would you use sub-headings to break up your text?

Benefits of sub-headings

1. Show relationship between ideas

Sub-headings allow a reader to see with one glance the topics or ideas within a document. They can see immediately the relationship between the ideas and then decide whether they want to read on or not.

2. Tell a story

Sub-headings tell a story on their own. They allow your reader to see the content and encourage them to read on further about the topic.

3. Highlight key points

Sub-headings are generally written in bold, larger font, underlined or italicized. Your main points are highlighted so your reader gets every chance to read your topic. There is a visual impact of sub-headings.

4. Increase focus

Using sub-headings within your text allows you to focus on your message. You will avoid repetition and remain focused on the sole topic of your paragraph(s).

How to use sub-headings

Here are a few tips when crafting and writing sub-headings:

1. Sub-headings should be specific

When you use headings, be as specific as you can. Don't be vague or your reader won't read your article. Instead of saying '*Sales to increase next year*', use '*25% increase in sales next year*'.

2. Sub-headings should be parallel

To get maximum impact from your sub-headings, your headings should be parallel. By that, I mean that they should have the same inflection, tone or style.

These sub-headings are parallel as they all start with verb:

- Increase market share
- Write great copy
- Grow sales now

These sub-headings aren't:

- Increasing market share
- Great copy written
- Grow sales now

3. Sub-headings should be fit for purpose

When writing sub-headings, make sure you discuss only what your headings suggest. If your sub-heading is about increasing sales in quarter one, don't digress and go into sales for quarter two. Make that point into another paragraph with it's own sub-heading.

No action today!

Today, there is no homework, except for the learning involved. Sub-headings are a great way to break up your text. Just be aware of their existence when planning your next copy. And then use them.

Day 14 - Forget Diamonds. Editing is the Writer's Best Friend

Forget diamonds. Editing is the writer's best friend. At the beginning of this book, I spoke about getting started and ways in which to avoid procrastinating. I advised you to start writing and gave you techniques to write better copy. Now that your text is written, it's time to start editing.

Writing is more than writing; putting words down on paper is just the start. Editing allows you to finesse your thoughts, your content, your style and tone and your spelling.

Many people confuse editing with doing a spellcheck. If they do a computer spellcheck or grammar check, then the document is edited. However, that's not the case. Editing is a process which includes a number of elements.

How to edit successfully

1. Step away from your document

I've heard it said that time is a great healer; equally so, time is a great editor. Once you've written your points down on paper (using the tips that I've discussed throughout this book), you should step away from the document.

Go to the cinema, have a coffee with a friend, hit the gym, pump some iron - whatever it is you do to relax, do it. Take at least a day away from the document or article. You need time to not think about it. Then when you go back to it, you'll see its strengths, weaknesses, gaps and errors.

2. Check the flow of your document

Go through every single sentence of text. Ask yourself '*and?*' at the end of every sentence. This '*and?*' makes you question the flow of two sentences, one leading to another. If it jars, then highlight it, go back & edit it.

3. Put yourself in your readers shoes

If you've been following the '*31 days to write better copy*' process, you'll have had the reader in mind from the beginning. However, at the editing process, now that the words are on paper, it's time to go back into your reader's shoes. Ask yourself such questions as:

- what does that word mean?
- what does the abbreviation mean?
- why didn't you say that to me earlier in the document?
- is there something missing in that sentence there?

Going through your text will allow you to be objective. You'll see things differently, such as words you thought you wrote but aren't actually there.

Checklist for Editing

For the purposes of this article, I'm using the word 'document' to describe anything that you write (newsletter, ezine, website, blog, whitepaper, press release, flyer).

Here are six items to check for when editing your text.

1. Aim of the document

It's time to revisit some key questions:

- What is the aim of the document?
- Who is the audience?
- What are you looking to say?
- What is the action that the reader must take after reading your document?

Often times, once you begin writing, the focus becomes blurred. That's totally fine, getting started is the key. Editing allows you to ask these questions again. Answer them with honesty.

2. The Content

Take a careful look at the content within the document. After reading through the document:

- Is all the right content there?
- Can you add something?
- Can you take something away?
- Do you need to explain something a bit more?

It's okay to add in extra content, just as it is to remove it. You need to have the right balance of content in order to engage with your reader.

3. The Layout

Copy structure (sub-headings, bulleted lists, numbering) helps with breaking up the text into readable chunks. Ask yourself:

- Do I have enough 'chunks' or paragraphs?
- Are some sentences too long? too short?
- Does your text need to be re-organized?
- Would one paragraph be better at the top than at the end?

When you edit, you may find yourself moving text around to make the document easier to read.

4. The Style & Tone

While style is quite personal as no two writers write the same, it is important to check for style and tone. Your document should flow using your style and tone.

- Are you mixing formal with informal language?
- Are you using the passive voice when the active voice could be used?
- Are you too specific in one section and vague in another?

5. The Language

Expanding on point no. 4 (style and tone), the language used should be consistent. Words and language is at the heart of every document. Ask yourself about your choice of words. Are some words:

- Out-dated
- Colloquial
- Irrelevant
- Unprofessional
- Too technical
- Not technical enough

Take a good look at the words that you use.

6. Grammar and spelling

Grammar and spelling are two errors that stand out to the reader straight away. You need to check that words are spelled properly and that the grammar is correct.

Like yesterday, there is no homework. HOWEVER, you should use this listing every single time you write something. It takes 21 days to form a habit so use it at least that many times until editing becomes second nature to you.

Day 15 - Be Careful with your Choice of Language

The words you choose within your written promotional material matter. Those words inform the reader, not only about the message you are trying to portray but also the kind of person you are. Depending on your medium, words should be chosen carefully.

A word can be defined as "*A sound or a combination of sounds, or its representation in writing or printing, that symbolizes and communicates a meaning and may consist of a single morpheme or of a combination of morphemes.*"*

The meaning that you want to give should be clear from your choice of words. If you're writing a proposal and want your writing to sound businesslike and professional, then avoid trendy words. If however, you're writing sales copy or an advert aimed at the youth market, then use trendy words and avoid business words.

If you want your writing to sound modern and contemporary, you should avoid out-dated words. If you want to sound friendly, then you should avoid formal text.

Buzzword bingo

I remember when I was working in the corporate world, there was a game that went around called '*Buzzword Bingo*'. (That's the polite version!). Here it is just one for you to play the next time you hear your government ministers talk on the radio!

It's a great game, but it shows you how certain words have become unfashionable, laughable and over-used.

Here is an example of one that you can play (when you're finished writing your copy!)

Out of the loop	Reap the rewards	At the end of the day	Think outside the box	Benchmark
Deliverable	Ball park figure	Bottom line	Back on track	Slippery slide
Customer Centric	Touch base	Take that offline	Value added	Quality management
Take stock	Brainstorm	Go the extra mile	Client Focused	Win-win situation
Leverage	Ground rules	First past the post	Strategic fit	Quick fix

Swinton, Lyndsay. "Buzz word bingo - play it and win!." Mftrou.com. 7 January 2007. < http://www.mftrou.com/buzz-word-bingo.html >.

Choosing the right words

Remember your target audience and your medium determines the use of words, but here are some general thoughts to consider.

1. Colloquial words

Colloquial words can be limited to a geographic area or used in informal chat. Generally speaking, colloquial words should not be included in professional or written writing. The exception to this is adverts or sales copy with a play on the words.

When I visited Dallas frequently for work years ago, the term 'y'all' or 'y'all y'all' was used all the time: "y'all going to d'vine for lunch?" Perfect question to ask over the phone but not on a document.

Colloquial words, such as *'yeah'*, *'you know'*, *'whatever'*, *'later'* or *'gonna'* should be avoided like the plague. In fact, sayings such as *'avoiding like the plague'* should be avoided too unless it's well known.

Be aware of the colloquial terms that you use in everyday speech and in your writing.

2. Outdated words

Unless you are writing for or to the legal profession, words from a past generation are considered out-dated. Your writing will read artificial and stilted. Find other words to use to sound less boring.

A few examples:

Herewith find attached my CV.
I am attaching.

As per your request, I have compiled a list of the top-sellers in our region.
As you requested, here is the list of top sellers.

I'll be there forthwith
I'll be there immediately

3. Over-used words

You know when you hear a song on the radio for the first time and you think it's great? Then after a while, it just grates on you. You turn it off when it comes on. Over-playing a song is just as bad for sales as under-playing it.

The same is true with your text. A couple of years back, '*going forward*' and '*synergy*' were buzzwords; they were the words of the 1990s. Now, they just seem old hat, everyone is saying them, to the point where they are a turn-off.

Think of the buzzword bingo and avoid such words.

4. Trendy words

Until a trendy or fad word is added to a dictionary, then it should be avoided in written, business communication.

You don't want to confuse your readers. While trendy terms (googling, tweeting) are perfectly understood by some of your audience, they may not be to others. Avoid alienating half your audience.

Action: Research words within your industry

In your industry or sector, draw up a list of words that you see regularly. Check out industry sites, industry journals, your competitors site and your own site.

- What are the trendy or 'trending' words within your industry?
- How many of them do you use?
- What technical words are 'de rigueur' in your industry?

Pick up the phone and ask your top three customers two questions:

1. What do they think the words mean

2. How relevant are they for them

3. How important are the words if they read them on your copy

Change your copy as a result of the conversation.

* Ask.com (http://www.ask.com/reference/dictionary/ahdict/53302/word)

Day 16 - Writing Styles, They are a Changing

I got this text recently from a beautician:

O4U. Gr8 offer 2day. B1,G1F all manicures. CMB 01 1234567

I blinked several times trying to understand it. I understood 'all manicures' and that was all. I had to show it to a friend's teenage son to make sense of it. He looked at it, translated it straight-away and looked at me as if I was 102 years old.

Translation:
Only for you. Great offer today. Buy one, get one free on all manicures. Call me back on 01 1234567.

I think I'm "down with the young people". Well obviously I'm not! Taking 20 minutes to realize I need help translating a message makes me feel old. And guess what? My beautician is older than me!

But I got to thinking about how much communication has changed over the last 10 years, let alone 50 or 100 years.

Change in business communication

The biggest change that has been made in business communication is writing style. The basic rules still apply such as good grammar, correct use of punctuation, structured sentences and flowing sentences. The style has changed enormously. It's less formal (even in professional communications), it's direct and isn't afraid to show a bit of emotion.

We've all changed our reading style - once we read cover to cover; now we glance using sub-headings, bullets and small paragraphs.

Long gone are pages of text when the shortest sentence was 20 words. Nowadays, we want information in short, succinct bites which are clear and cogent.

What you need to do as a writer is convey your message correctly to your audience. Your writing style needs to appeal to your audience.

Acknowledge your writing style and adapt it to your audience. I'm not advocating that you send text messages like the one I received. The basics of copywriting are still there - you're looking for the sale or the piqued interest in your product. Adapt your writing style and ensure it's appropriate to your audience.

Action: Assess your writing style

Take the rest of the day to assess your writing style. Go back to documents that you've written before. (They are there on your computer, believe me!).

- Is your writing style different now than before?
- Is your writing style appropriate to your audience?
- Do you have more than one writing style depending on your audience segmentation?
- Do you know what style your audience likes to read?
- (If not, then go back to Day 1 and 2 to do a bit more research)

Be aware of your writing style the next time you sit down to write promotional copy.

Day 17 – How to Write a Great P.S. Statement

The P.S. or post-script is often said to be the second most important part of the sales letter after the headline. With this in mind, I did a small sample survey of my friends and colleagues about the P.S. statement. Over 90% of respondents said that they glance at it while some (15%) really take the time to read it.

While this little survey is by no means quantifiable or statistical, it does show that the average reader reads the P.S. statement.

Given that people are generally time-poor and reading has become glancing, here are five things to think about when writing an effective P.S. statement to suit your business.

1. Emphasize action

When you write direct responses sales letters, the call to action is so important. With your P.S. statement, you can emphasize that the reader must act now to avail of time limited bonus or special offer. It's all about picking up the phone now and placing the order or finding out more about you.

2. Restate benefits

Write a one liner summarizing your product's main benefit and why the reader really needs it. People buy for two reasons - they want a problem solved or the product/service produces a certain feeling or emotional response. Remind them why your product/service is the best product or service on the market.

3. Explain your guarantee

If you talk about a guarantee on your sales letter, you can restate it here. Explain why you are giving the guarantee (relationship building etc) and tell them that you are absorbing the risk. Tell your readers that buying your product is a no-brainer - it's a win-win for all.

4. Redefine your unique selling point

Take the time to write a line about what makes you different. Why should someone buy from you over someone else. If it's credibility that a reader is looking for, state it. If it's success stories, give details of some. Whatever makes you different to your competitor, restate it here.

5. Don't go overboard

Think about using the P.S. statement as giving that final push for sales but remember, too many P.S. or P.P.S statements make you look desperate for the sale. Don't waste the last opportunity to make or break the sale. Make the sale by thinking carefully about your P.S. Statement.

Action: Write a P.S. statement for your last sales letter

Grab the last sales letter you wrote. Take another look at it.

- What words can you use to write a P.S. Statement?
- What is the final final word that you'd like to tell your customer.
- Write a P.S. Statement here

Day 18 - How to Use Call to Action in your Sales Literature

A call to action is the term to get your reader to do something after reading your letter. Every sales document that you write should have a strong call to action. This includes your sales letter, your website, your blog page, your newsletter. There are a number of benefits to using a call to action for both you and your reader.

Benefits to using call to actions

Benefits to You:

1. It helps you focus on your sales pitch.
2. It makes you limit your sales page to one offer.

Benefits to Your Reader :

1. It provides closure on the subject.
2. It directs your reader to take a specific action.

Four tips to writing call to action statements

1. Be clear

Don't confuse your reader with too many call to actions so they don't know what to do. Too many options can be off-putting to your reader.

2. Offer a little something

Sometimes you have to give a little encouragement to your reader to get them to take your call to action. A free ebook, a trial period, free shipping, entry to a competition or a discount. A human characteristic that we all share (even secretly) is that we hate to miss something. That's why a time limit often works.

3. Use strong language

If you were lost in a forest, you'd want to hear decisive words, not weak murmurs. Which directions would you follow:

"Take a left by the big oak tree, jump over the river and run."
or
"Skip over to that tree, stop and look around, then decide which direction looks more appealing."

You should use strong language that offers value. Don't pussy-foot, tell your reader what you'd like them to do.:

- Call us
- Order now
- Sign up
- Subscribe here
- Register now

4. Have a Call to Action on every page

Don't limit yourself to one call to action on your website. Make sure, that you have a call to action on each page.

Remember that every page is a landing page.

Action: Write five call to action statements

Click on five web pages that are bookmarked on your browser.

- Do they have a call to action?
- If not, can you write one for them?
- If yes, would you take the action asked of you? Why? Why not?
- What would you change about the call to action?

Day 19 - The Role of Emotion in Copywriting

Emotion plays a huge part in the buying process. You've all heard the saying "*My heart says yes but my head says no.*" What you need to do as a successful copy-writer is get inside the head of the buyer and encourage them to buy with their heart and head.

Check out the following scenario. Two people are chatting across the wall of their gardens chit-chatting about nothing really. The topic turns to cars. One neighbor says to the other:

"*Ah, yeah, I'd like a new car next year, but we'll see how things go.*"

But you know what he's really saying "*I want the new Audi A1 in silver metallic and I've placed my order already.*"

Add another dimension to this thought-process:

"*I want the new Audi A1 in silver metallic which will look better in the driveway than your (last year's!) Mercedes CLS.*"

Neighbor No. 2 goes into the house and shouts to the wife, "*Honey, we're getting a new car.*"

Sound believable?

Yes.

That's because it is. Neighbor no. 1 could have bought any car. He didn't. He chose the new Audi A1. (Reward for working so hard, pride, delight).

He could have told the neighbor that he placed an order but didn't. (Wants to see surprise on neighbor face, greed, one-upmanship).

Neighbor No. 2 reads between the lines and tells the wife that they're getting a new car. (one-upmanship, vanity, fear of losing face to the neighbor next door).

Everyone buys on emotion

People buy from people and people buy as people. It doesn't matter if they are buying a pair of shoes, a jacket, dinner or a multi-million pound computer system. People buy to fulfill an emotional need. Thereafter, they rationalize their decisions.

The pair of shoes

I have an important meeting and don't have navy shoes to match the navy suit that makes me look very professional and credible.

The jacket

It has an inside pocket which will allow me to carry my business cards and do more networking.

The dinner

Everyone has to eat, right? Plus it's healthy and has so many salads to choose from.

The multi-million pound computer system

There will be less human-error so less time having to deal with screaming, disappointed customers.

You need to find out what the triggers the emotions within your target market. The only way to find out is do what I talked to you about on Day 1 - Understanding your customer. The more you find out about your customer or target market, the easier it will be to persuade them that your product or service is the right one for them.

Emotional triggers

Emotional triggers include:

- Fear
- Delight
- Approval
- Laziness

- Curiosity

In fact, you could use the seven deadly sins as reasons why people buy:
- Envy
- Pride
- Greed
- Wrath
- Lust
- Sloth
- Gluttony

Taking a positive spin

While the seven deadly sins are deadly for a reason (and we all saw that in the movie Se7en with Brad Pitt and Morgan Freeman), I would encourage you to focus on the positive.

So if vanity or greed are emotional triggers within your market, try discussing the benefits of your product or service. Take a positive spin on your product. If you say something like '*Don't be like everyone else, buy this*"; it really means "*You'll be like everyone else if you buy this.*" Our sub-conscious really can't digest negatives. How many times have you walked on the grass when you saw the sign '*Don't walk on the grass.*'

Exactly! All the time. You saw '*walk on the grass!*'. Turn the emotional trigger into a positive. You could say something like this for a tanning product: '*Buy our tanning product and people will think you're just back from holidays*' or '*Get that 'just home' look with our tanning product.*'

Here, you are creating a positive association with your product. People always want to remember their holidays - that relaxed feeling, the healthy tan, the adventurous glow. And if your target market is a little bit vain, well, then, they'll think they're a little better than the average orange-tanned beauty.

You're playing into their emotional response of looking good, looking better than the next person while thinking about their holiday. You've got a sale.

Action: Does your industry have emotions?

As human beings, we have emotional reactions to all kinds of things. What are your target market's reactions?

If you don't know, go and ask three of your customers the following question:

If they had all the money in the world, what would they do differently in their business and at home?

Jot the answers down here to find a common theme. The answers are the emotional triggers which you have to include in your next copy piece.

Day 20 - Features and Benefits - What's your Take?

It's the age old marketing dilemma. Which elements of your business do you promote? The features, the benefits or both?

I've seen many, many documents which detail only the features. Business owners or marketing executives who live and breathe their product and service often get caught up with the features of the product, how wonderful they are, how they differentiate their product from the competitors.

So they write information about how fantastic the product is and elaborate on the features. But as I discussed in Day 19, emotion plays a huge part in the buying process.

People buy because of the benefits of the product, not the features. Yes, the features are important but it's the pain that buyers are concerned about. Can you alleviate the pain or not? They don't really care if it's in a white bottle, pink bottle, blue bottle or a tub. The question is how fast you can relieve the pain.

When you're really excited about a product, sometimes you assume that benefits of your product or service are so obvious that they don't need to be stated. You're super excited about the multi-spray garden hose that you invented and you just can't wait to tell people about it.

You think that automatically everyone will see the benefit of a multi-spray garden hose. You know you do so you begin talking about the wonderful features of it – the length of hose, the nozzle, the attachment to the tap or faucet.

Yet often times you need to be specific and tell people about the benefits, not just leave it up to assumptions.

What are features?

Features are the nuts and bolts of a product or service. It's the engine, the accelerator, the steering wheel. It's all the bits you can see and touch and feel and smell. It's the facts of the product.

What are benefits?

Benefits are the intangible. It's the feeling you get when you use something. It's the answer to the 'So What?' question. It's the reason why you buy the car with the BMW badge. It's the warm and fuzzy sense you get when you assess the product.

Feature v benefit examples

Here are some examples to get your teeth into writing your own features and benefits:

Vacuum Cleaner

Feature: Comes complete with a 5metre tube

Benefit: Reaching those hard to reach corners is a thing of the past with the 5metre tube

Mobile Phone

Feature: 15 number speed dial

Benefit: Reducing time and keystrokes calling your favorite numbers

Dog Kennels

Feature: Open 365 days a year

Benefit: You can now go on holidays

I heard John Carlton, the guru of copywriting once say that men write features, women write benefits. He often gets copy from women and after reading pages and pages, he is still unclear about what the product or service is, but he knows how he'll feel when he buys it!

I thought that was rather funny, because no matter what you're selling, you do need to include both features and benefits.

Action: Assess your competitor's website for features and benefits

Today, I want you to look at your competitors websites. Read their home page, their services or product page and their news page.

Assess whether their content is feature-laden? Is it written with the customer in mind? Are the benefits clear?

What do you notice? Jot down your notes here.

Day 21 - Email Etiquette - The Dos and Don'ts of Emailing

We each receive hundreds of emails a week. It has become the communication method of choice for many business professionals. It is easy to sit down and write an email and another one and another one. Sometimes it simply is more efficient than picking up the telephone.

However, just as face-to-face first impressions last, so too do email impressions. You can't take back an email sent in haste or you can't laugh off the joke that insulted someone (even though that wasn't your intention).

Email communication can be difficult to get right. As it is a communication method, it has all the attributes necessary for good communication - sender encodes the message and the receiver decodes message - but as the writer isn't in front of the reader, the message can often get decoded incorrectly.

Generally speaking, there are seven elements to the communications process:

1. The Sender sends a message
2. The message is encoded by the sender
3. The message is received by the receiver

4. The message is decoded by the receiver
5. The receiver gives a response or feedback back to the sender
6. This feedback or response is encoded
7. This feedback or response is decoded.

Every step can get 'infected' by noise. This noise might be an internal response by the receiver, a message being received at the wrong time or sheer volume of email traffic and demands on the receiver.

As such, you must step into the shoes of your reader (as much as possible) when writing your message.

Reasons for email etiquette

Some organizations have a formal email policy, others operate on an informal basis. Some employees or business owners set their own standards when setting emails. Whatever you do, try to have your own email etiquette based on the following values:

1. Professionalism

Above all, your emails should represent you in a positive and professional light. You wouldn't wear a dirty, creased suit to work so you shouldn't send an email that portrays a less-than positive image of yourself.

2. Clarity

Be as clear as you can with your emails. Say what you need to say and sign off.

3. Approachability

You are neither everyone's best friend nor are you their boss. Be approachable in your emails; don't be over-friendly and don't be too cold. Find yourself a happy medium as emails do help to build and nurture relationships.

Dos of emailing

- **Do** think carefully about what you want to write
- Write your emails when you are calm or in a neutral mood.

- **Do** use sub-headings, bulleted or numbering lists to break up text
- If you need to write a long email, then break up the text into readable chunks.

- **Do** edit your emails
- As I mentioned earlier in the book, time is a great healer. It allows you time to re-read your email and change a phrase or delete an emotionally charged rant on an email.

- **Do** use a corporate email policy
- If there is a policy in your organization, find it and use it. If there isn't one, set about writing your own one. Like this one, list out a few dos and don'ts so that all corporate emails follow a similar pattern.

- **Do** find out how your reader likes his emails
- If your reader prefers small emails, write small, to-the-point emails. If he likes a bit of chit-chat, ask after the family. If she prefers an informal tone, talk to her as if she is a friend.

- **Do** use a script or template for frequently asked questions
- If you constantly find yourself replying to the same or similar questions, craft a response and use it.

Don'ts of emailing

- **Don't** hit the 'send' button without reading or proofing your written email
- You can't take an email back so double check your email. Ensure there is no hidden agenda or insult.

- **Don't** over-use emotion icons
- :-) ;-) are all very well and good to help convey a message. But if your emails are consistently filled with these icons, your

reader will get annoyed. It will show that you can't express yourself using the written word.

- **Don't** digress
- Make a point in your email and stick to it. Don't digress on another point or write long-winded text where the reader can't find your point.

- **Don't** write IN CAPITALS
- Capitals infer screaming. It's not professional and can appear arrogant and insulting. If you want to highlight a point, use underline, italics, bold, color or center alignment.

- **Don't** use incorrect words
- Urgent, important, reply today are words that you see regularly in emails. Many times, they are used to engender a response. But ask yourself how urgent or important is your email to your sender before using the words

Action: Does your organization have an email policy?

It's time to find out if your organization has an email policy.

If not, write a five point email policy based on the above information, taking into account your organizational culture.

Day 22 - Writing Effective Email Subject Lines

What's the point of writing a fantastic email when no-one opens it? It's like owning a shop and watching people walk by your door, day in, day out. It can get weary and in the end, you give up trying to entice them into your shop. You close the door and walk away. The same thing could happen to you with your email marketing campaigns. You give them up. Before you do that, you need to take a better look at your email subject line.

Meeting expectations

To order to encourage people to open your email, you need an enticing subject line that matches their expectations. A lot of people who mail don't really think about expectations. They just want to communicate, build a relationship or get a sale.

Think about where you got your email listing from. Did you buy it? Did you grow it organically? Did you offer a free report? Did you offer a 20% discount off the first purchase?

The answers to the questions matter.

- If your newsletter listing prefers a 'soft-sell', then use subject lines that offer advice.

- If your newsletter listing prefers a 'hard-sell', then offer discounts.

Match your subject line with the expectations of the group. If you have to segment your database, segment it. You will see an automatic response in your open rates.

Length of subject line

The general rule of thumb is that your subject line should be fifty characters or less. The one for today's article is 48 characters. 50 characters isn't much, is it?

This is where you need to plan your emails...whether they are for a promotion, email newsletter or a simple one-to-one email that needs an answer.

You need to work your email around your 50-character-or-less subject line. That way, you'll really focus on the subject line and not just write it as an after-thought.

5 tips to write effective email subject lines

In order to avoid your email hitting the email dustbin, here are a few tips to write effective email campaigns.

1. 50-characters-or-less mantra

Keep focusing on the 50 characters. If you focus on the 50 characters, you will highlight the most important fact of the email. It's tough to do initially and it does take practice. It is easier to write "*'31 Days to Write Better Copy' book Deemed a Success*" than "*Copywriting program run-away success*".

'31 Days to Write Better Copy' book Deemed a Success : 53 characters

Copywriting Program Run-Away Success : 39 characters

It takes time to condense your thoughts into 50 characters. Just keep practising and focusing on the 50-characters-or-less rule.

2. Test your subject lines

Just because you start every newsletter with the same thing (e.g.) *'Denisefay.com Newsletter'*, doesn't mean you have to do it all the time. Change it around and test it. People like variety, even if they've come to expect the same thing from you. Change one word or one phrase at a time.

3. Use curiosity with a deadline

We all hate to miss something. As social beings, we want to be included or at least know what's going on. Magazine shelves are covered with magazines telling us about the lives of others. Use this curiosity connected with time on your subject line. "*Order tonight by midnight or miss out.*", "*3 days left until...*", "*You've got 6 hours left before the...*"

It's a 'keeping up with the Jones' approach and it works. (Bearing in mind the expectations of your newsletter database.)

4. Be careful with certain words

'*Free*' used to be the number one word that people responded to - they hit the delete button. Especially if it was accompanied by several exclamation points or written in all uppercase. However, don't dismiss 'free' - it is still a useful word that can be used within a good sentence. You just have to remember who are emailing to.

Other words to be careful of are '*percent off*' and '*reminder*'. Again, it goes to expectations of your email newsletter database. Sometimes these words can appear too salesy, too pushy and offensive.

5. Subject line must match content

If you test regularly and know what your readers are expecting, then don't write a subject line that you know they'll open but have content they'll hate. You need to stay true to the content and the subject line.

Action: Time to go into your email box

Go into your email box and look at the emails that were sent to you over the past 24 hours. What characteristics do they share? Take a look at:

- Their length
- The first word
- The sentence structure
- The topic
- Your interest in the subject line

What action would you take with each of these emails? All are urgent and all are looking for your time. If you had 15 minutes, which ones would you open, file or delete within that 15 minutes?

Use this information when you go to write your next email.

Day 23 - Content is King on the Internet

The Internet is called the superhighway for a reason. It is full of information and content. You can find any amount of content on any subject that you want. It's the reason why we all go online - to read, to watch or listen to a video or to find out more about a particular topic.

Yet so many websites are simply cluttered with images that you don't read the content. You look at the lovely pictures and move on.

This short article makes the point that content is king. You need to prioritize it before you create your graphics. So many websites are built around an image, leaving little room for content, the holy grail of search engine optimization.

Content is king

Content is king on any website. Think of it this way - content is your virtual salesman, business owner or shop assistant. It sells your product. And just as you have shelves, menu cards or mannequins in your shop supporting the product, you have images on your website.

How many times have you walked into a shop with the most fantastic shelves but nothing on them? You don't. You'll go into the shop when the shelves are full.

It's the same online. Graphics support your content. Every business has it's own supports and on the Internet, graphics and images support your content.

Content and graphics work together

Layout of text and graphics is very important. There really is nothing worse than a text-laden page. Similarly there is nothing worse than a page with lots of images and no content to browse.

The two work well together. A picture tells a thousand words so you need graphics, images or animations to brighten up your text. Just prioritize on the content.

People visit your site again and again because they want to read the content that you have - your blog, articles, opinions, whitepapers, interviews. Also the search engines love content. They send their spiders to websites with good, useful content. They don't send their spiders to sites which have little content and lots of images.

Action: How many images do you have?

I ask my clients how many images they have on their website. Many don't know because the web designer *"looks after all that."*

So today, go to your website. Look at the main pages. How many images do you have? Have they a name? Do they support your content or do they distract from it?

Ask a customer or family member what they think about the images on your website. Get their feedback on the balance of images and content.

Day 24 - Measuring Copy Effectiveness

I know what it's like. You spend hours researching your target market to find out what exactly they want to read and what language they prefer to use. You write your copy, edit it and write it again. You're not going to publish it until you are 100% happy and proud that the document that you have just written is spot on.

Once you've decided what to write and who you're writing to, you need to decide on measurability. There really is no point putting so much effort into writing without thinking about how you're going to measure the success of your copy.

People measure their written material in a number of different ways. This article gives you a number of ways by which you can measure the effectiveness and success of your copy.

1. Readability score of your copy

There are a number of methods to measure the readability of your copy. The most commonly used formula is the Flesch formula. Designed by Rudolph Flesch in 1948, it provides a Reading Ease Score. In a nutshell, it analyzes how easy or difficult your text is to read.

The formula for the Flesch Reading Ease Score (FRES) test is:

$$206.876 - 1.015\left(\frac{total\ words}{total\ sentences}\right) - 84.6\left(\frac{total\ syllables}{total\ words}\right)$$

Basically, it analyses four elements:

1. Average number of words per sentence
2. Average word length (number of syllables per 100 words)
3. Percentages of personal words
4. Percentages of personal sentences.

The Reading Ease scores vary from 0 to 100, with 0 being incredibly difficult to read and 100 really easy. According to Wikipedia, The Reader's Digest magazine has a readability index of about 65, Time magazine scores about 52, and the Harvard Law Review has a general score in the low 30s.

The relationship between FRES and difficulty goes something like this:

Very difficult	Below 30
Difficult	30-49
Average	50-79
Easy	80-89
Very easy	90 and above

The Flesch formula is not without it's idiosyncrasies. It analyzes longer text rather than shorter copy and takes colloquial phrases into account. However, it does highlight what us copywriters have been saying for years - shorter sentences with short words are easy to read and understand.

For a bit of fun, I checked the above section on the website - Readability Formulas (://www.readabilityformulas.com/free-readability-formula-assessment.php)

It gave me a Flesch Reading Ease of 63.97. So, similar to the Reader's Digest; not bad, eh?!

2. Call to action count

If you've followed my advice and tips through-out this book, you will know that you need to have a call to action on every piece of material that you've written. Your call to actions can (and should) include the following:

- an opt-in to a newsletter
- pick up the phone to buy
- email the sales team
- click to another page
- write a comment
- forward to a friend

Now, count how many call to actions were taken within a given time period.

You can work out your conversion rate to calculate the copy's call to action effectiveness. Say you wrote and sent 100 flyers with a strong discount call to action and 20 people bought your product. Well, that's a conversion rate of 20%, which is very good.

The same conversion ratio can be applied to a website. If you had a newsletter opt-in on your home page with 200 people hitting your homepage and only 3 people subscribed, well that's a conversion rate of 1.5%.

If you are not happy with the conversion rates, it's time to tweak, change or edit your copy. But remember to change one thing at a time; else you won't know what change made the difference in the increase of call to action items or conversion rates.

3. Advertising measurables

If you have a few written promotions on-going at the same time, i.e., a webpage and a mailshot, then you need ways to track where the call to actions are coming from. Here are some ideas to differentiate the call to action while still keeping an eye on the overall copy effectiveness:

- Use two different names in your campaigns
- Use a different telephone number for each campaign

You can still analyze your conversion rates as per No. 2 above but at least you can differentiate the results.

Action: What are your objectives?

The task today is more a subjective task. I want you to remind yourself what your objectives are for your website and your promotional literature. If you didn't have objectives, other than to promote yourself, then that's fine but that will have to change. Everything should be measurable.

If you set objectives, were they met? Did you achieve what you set out to achieve?

For your website, if you have no clear objectives, then I want you to write some down now. Here are some prompts:

- Increase traffic?
- Increase credibility?
- Get sales?
- Generate sales?
- Encourage an opt-in?

Day 25 - Elements of a Content Strategy

For the past 24 chapters, I've talked about understanding your audience, writing structured sentences, breaking up your copy into readable/glanceable (if there is such a word!) chunks.

The tips and advice all apply in practice to any and every written promotional method. With all the different types, it's hard to know what to prioritize; which will bring the better return for your business.

Creating your content strategy

At this stage of the program, now that you know how to write, you should be thinking of creating your own content strategy. What methods are you going to use to promote your business? There are many, many ways to promote your business using the written word and in this article, I'm only touching the surface.

If you could engage some or all of these, then we can move onto phase 2 of your content strategy - using webinars, podcasts and videos. I'd recommend mastering certain elements of your strategy first. There is almost a 'conquer and master' logic. Get to grips with some, build them into your content strategy and introduce a new element. You could try one a new element a month but do what is right for you.

Elements of a content strategy

Based on my experience as a copy-writer, here is the list of the most popular elements that clients ask me to write. I've included the advantages and disadvantages of each element, based on my own and my client's experience. Writing isn't easy, so be prepared for the disadvantages aswell as the advantages of each element.

Here are some items that should be in your content strategy. There are others but this will get you started!

Element	Description	Advantages	Disadvantages
Article	A piece of text generally over 300 words, written on a specific topic.	Builds your credibility as expert in your field. Brings traffic to your site.	Time-consuming to write and edit. Need to write a few to see the benefits.
Ezines	Email newsletter sent to internal database of customers, prospects, friends, interested	Monitor interest on topics with click-through rates. Keeps you in-front of customer. Great for soft-selling. Builds your	De-motivating if newsletter not opened or no click-throughs. Time-consuming to make sure it reads well on different emails systems. Need to

	parties. Contains at least two articles - welcome and information re product or service.	credibility if you give free advice. If hard-selling, can produce actual sales.	send emails regularly so requires commitment.
Newsletter	Physical newsletter sent to internal database of customers, prospects, friends, interested parties. Contains several articles of interest to the reader.	Differentiator as most people send email newsletters. Good relationship-building too. Can result in sales depending on product/service.	Expensive as have print and postage costs. Requires commitment to send regularly (monthly, quarterly, half-yearly).
Website	Holy grail of your Internet presence. Is	Promotes your business online. Gives people a	em...Only one is that it is time-consuming. You

	your shop-front to the world.	sense of who you are. Sales-making tool if you have ecommerce capabilities.	need to constantly update your website to make it relevant to users and search-engines.
Blog	Blog is an online log of your activities. A diary if you will. In this context, it's a professional record of your ideas, knowledge, events etc. Blog can be anything from 1 to 5 paragraphs.	Great for driving traffic to your site. Sharing ideas or events is easy. Builds credibility as a professional. Interesting way to promote your thoughts.	Need to write at least one a week so commitment needed. Often after initial investment, the writer or blogger runs out of ideas that they think are interesting. Hard to stay motivated.
Whitepapers	A white-paper is a long document that is generally technical in	Highlights competency in specialist area. Builds enormous credibility if	Not suitable for every industry.

	nature but highlights your expertise in an area. Generally more than four pages.	written in engaging way. Good promotional tool for using as 'opt-in'.	
Case-studies	Case-studies are documents which showcase your product or service in action. Should be 1-2 pages with quotes from client.	Great as part of your press kit and as a download on your website. Fantastic to highlight your product or service in action.	The only disadvantage is the time involved. There can be 'back and forward' with client for approval.
Corporate Brochure	A brochure that highlights your company, it's product or services. Generally handed to customers/pros	Provides further information on your product or service after meeting. Great for showcasing your products/services	Can be costly as to do it right, you need a designer. Depending on your organization, approval through various channels can be time-

	pects at meeting. Can be anything from two pages to 20 pages, depending on layout.	or case-studies.	consuming.
Flyers	One or two sided information sheet that directly sells a product.	Useful for promoting a product or service. Works well with a discount.	Can be costly as includes print and maybe post or door drop company. Can't be used in isolation, need to send them out regularly.

A word of advice. Don't give up. It can take 12 months to reap the rewards of your content strategy. It is hard, and if you need help, get help. But don't give up. You will see the return...it's just not immediate.

Action: Create your own content marketing strategy

Write down what elements of a content marketing strategy you are currently using. Ask yourself how regular you write? Is it enough? Be honest.

Now, pick one element from the listing above that you are going to start at the beginning of the next month. Thereafter, introduce one every month.

Write your future content strategy plan on a month by month basis.

Day 26 - 9 Steps to Writing a Successful Sales Script

When I was creating the curriculum for this program, the subject of sales scripts cropped up. I was talking with a client and he wanted to know, could I or would I write a sales script so that his team would have more success 'getting their foot in the door.'

They are tough to call, sales scripts. I mean, who hasn't experienced that false cheeriness and false sincerity on a call. There really is nothing worse than getting a sales call whereby you can actually feel the phoniness oozing down the phone from the get-go.

These days, people are making more cold calls and are selling themselves more at networking events. And on the flip side, I think more business owners are prepared to listen to people making cold calls.

I will still say that sincerity, research and knowledge pays off before you talk to anyone - whether it's on a document, on the phone or face to face.

Why use a sales script?

There are a number of reasons why sales scripts should be used. Here are the three main ones.

1. Focus

The main reason that someone should write and use a script is for focus. It allows a person to focus their thoughts and focus on what they want from the phone call or face to face encounter.

2. Control

It also allows you to control the conversation. Not in a dogmatic way but a way that allows you to guide the conversation. So perhaps guide is a better word than control!

3. Avoidance

You will avoid that 'doh!' moment when you hang up or walk away and realise that you forgot to ask an important question. It's so easy to do; you get drawn into conversation that you forget to ask some all-important question

Types of script

While I've mentioned telephone script here, there are times outside of a cold call where scripts are useful. These include:

- Networking script
- Referral script
- Presentation script
- Video script
- 'Pick your brain' script

Writing a sales script

1. Go back to basics

Before you begin to write a script, I want you to go back to basics. Revisit Day 1 and Day 2. These resources will help you focus on the writing for and researching of your audience. While a sales script is generally delivered orally, you need to be prepared.

2. Write the way you talk

I mentioned earlier in the article about that false cheeriness you often get with sales staff. Do they really care if I'm having a really bad day? No!

So if you don't normally get on the phone and ask "How are you today on this fine sunny day? Is it sunny over there in (insert location)?", then don't do it if you're selling your product.

Be natural.

3. Always get and give a name

Look for the person's name that you are talking to? I will always chat to someone using their name. It's so important, it's an almost instant connection.

4. Prepare a one sentence opener

Marketing and sales consultants regularly ask their clients or prospects about their unique selling point. Why? Because it focuses on what makes you different to the supplier up the street.

After you've introduced yourself, you need something that makes you stand out. And what better way to do that is to tell the truth about yourself and what it is you do.

5. Talk about benefits

When creating your one-liner, mention benefits not features. A person at the other end of the phone couldn't care less that you're next door, tell them what you do to make their life better. They don't need another nice neighbor!

You're the expert in your field so tell them that and why they should listen to you on this call.

6. Know the jargon

Every industry has certain words applicable to that industry. These jargon phrases should be used when making your call. But have a clear understanding about them. Don't use if you don't know what they mean.

7. Have a case-study ready

Usually I write case-studies which are 2 pages long, but I don't think your prospect wants to hear a case-study that long.

Use a case-study to tell your prospect that a similar business has engaged your services. This creates instant credibility because you know their industry and other businesses have 'tried you first'.

8. Keep the conversation fluid

Keep the conversation fluid. I've spoken quite a lot about the flow of a written document during these 31 days and the same applies to your script. Make sure that it flows and your conversation is a natural one. Okay, so it is a sales conversation but it can be natural. Stay away from the phoniness and insincerity.

9. Ask for what you want

Whether it is an appointment, a meeting, further contact details, a sale - ask for it. Your prospect isn't a mind reader and while you might be leading up to the ask, they don't know what it is until you ask for it. Be natural, be polite and be firm.

A good script allows you to say what you want to say, clearly and concisely, with room to have a natural flow to your conversation. Focus on your message and your audience - focusing on one without the other can make your call too salesy, pushy, phoney and ultimately you will be dismissed.

Action: Write your own sales script

Now it's time for you to think about how you approach a sale or a lead. Have you something scripted in your head or written down? Do you need to focus a bit more on your telephone calls? What about your networking pitch?

Take time today to follow the nine steps above to write a sales script. Your sales script should be fluid and natural. Own it.

Practice it on your team, family and friends to fine-tune it and get feedback.

Day 27 - The Magic Formula of Copywriting

I often get asked about the magic words to use when writing copy. Magic formulas don't exist. They don't exist in real life; they don't exist in copywriting.

There is no get-rich-quick scheme when it comes to writing. It comes down to what I talked about in Day 1 - get to know your audience, find out what they want and talk to them using the language that they like.

Connecting with your audience requires _you_. Your ability to engage, your voice, your personality, your choice of words. You need to talk to your reader as if you were talking to them face-to-face.

Once you have the fundamentals in place, then you can look at your language - the words that motivate and the words that are down right insulting.

Words that are proven to get results

The following is a list of words that have been proven to be motivators. They don't replace the copy that you have researched and wrote. They simply supplement it.

abolish	increase	realize
achieve	intensify	respect
blind-spot	jacked up	retain
build	knuckle	save
challenging	lifeblood	shatter
confidential	luxury	surreal
destiny	maximize	tactics
define	monumental	tap into
ensure	no sweat	train
explosive	novel	understand
find	opportunities	up close and personal
fundamentals	obsession	vulnerable
generate	persuade	whittle down
gut feeling	profit	win
hard facts	prevent	you
Hollywood	quiver	

Action: How many motivating words do you have?

There is no homework as such today. What I would like you to do today is go back to your own copy and see if you are using any of the motivating words.

Come back to this list again and again when you write your own promotional copy.

Day 28 - A Rough Guide to Grammar

Grammar is one of the hardest things to get right when you're writing an academic paper or a report to the boss. Copy, on the other hand, is a bit more forgiving. Promotional material that makes up copy is all about readability. Your material should relate to the reader, build a rapport and be engaging. Simple as that.

Grammar helps you to add clarity to your writing. Just remember the purpose of grammar is to assist your reader with understanding your message and taking an action afterwards.

Most of the grammar that you were taught in school still applies but times have changed since then...no matter what age you are! Unless you're writing to a professor or your old English teacher, you don't need to follow the letter of the law precisely with grammar.

Here are some basic grammar rules that you must apply when writing copy. I regularly see mistakes with these six items when editing copy.

1. a, an

Many people write with the belief that *a* goes before a word that starts with a consonant and *an* goes before a word that begins with a vowel. However, the use of *a* or *an* isn't determined by the first letter, it's actually determined by it's sound.

Think about it. Which reads better:

- He was given an honorary degree
- He was given a honorary degree

- I gave him a utility bill
- I gave him an utility bill

- We have a one-year old son
- We have an one-year old son.

It's very important to read your document back to yourself, outloud if possible. That way you hear, and see, the readability of your document.

The correct versions are:
- He was given *an* honorary degree
- I gave him *a* utility bill
- We have *a* one-year old son

2. Subject verb order

Generally sentences follow a structured order: subject-verb-object.

- I write promotional material
- She is an entrepreneur
- He runs marathons
- They answer the phones

Sometimes however, to make the text more engaging or to emphasize a point, the subject-verb-object order is changed. The verb appears before the subject. Be careful of using the reversed order as the sentence can appear cumbersome. Also, you could use the plural and singular use of the verb incorrectly.

Cumbersome Sentence

Continuing to be well received is the program, 31 days to write better copy, by an increasing audience.

You will see that the verb (continues) precedes the subject (the program) and object (audience).

Always think about your audience when you write and how they'll read the sentence. A better way to change the sentence is:

The program, 31 days to write better copy, continues to be widely read on a daily basis.

Plural or singular

Enclosed is my Curriculum Vitae and referee details.

The subject (Curriculum Vitae and referee details) and the verb (is) do not match. Curriculum Vitae and referee details are joint subjects and therefore the plural version of the verb should be used.

It should read:

*Enclosed **are** my Curriculum Vitae and referee details.*

Think about it in the verb-subject-object approach if you get confused,e.g., *My Curriculum Vitae and referee details **are** enclosed.*

It will help determine whether the verb takes the plural or singular version.

3. Contractions

Contractions are where we combine two words to make them one using an apostrophe.

- **He will** becomes ***He'll***
- **She is** becomes ***She's***
- **I am** becomes ***I'm***

In copy, contractions are allowed because they sound like the way we talk. Using **I am** or **he is** can often seem quite stilted or formal. Use contractions depending on your style of text.

4. It's or Its

Leading on from contractions, the main one you'll encounter is *it's* or *its*.

It's is a contraction of '*it is*.'
Its is possessive, just like his or hers, generally for an inanimate object or collective.

Take the following sentences:

"It's my intention to reduce the workforce by 10%." said the CEO.
Contraction: **It is** *my intention*

X industries to reduce workforce: The company announced at a press conference of its intention to reduce the workforce by 10%.
Possessive: **Company** *announced* **its** *intention*

If you're still not sure, think of it like this:
X industries to reduce workforce: The **CEO** *announced at a press conference of* **his** *intention to reduce the workforce by 10%.*

5. affect, effect

Two words that have different meanings yet are used inter-changeably for the wrong reasons.

Affect is a verb

Effect is a noun

Think about the two words in terms of other words to get the meaning right.

- Affect can be replaced with change
- Effect can be replaced with result

Let's look at the following sentences to see the difference between **effect** and **affect**:

- Her attitude was *affected* by the redundancies.
- Her attitude was *changed* by the redundancies.
- Her attitude was *resulted* by the redundancies.

- The *effect* of the redundancies will be reduced staff-morale.
- The *result* of the redundancies will be reduced staff-morale.
- The *change* of the redundancies will be reduced staff-morale

Replacing *'affected'* with *'resulted'* and *'effect'* with *'change'* changes the entire meaning of the sentences. They don't make sense and remember grammar is supposed to add clarity to your message.

6. Starting sentences with And & But

These were no-nos when I went to school. However, we start phonetic sentences with **but & and**, so the same applies when writing copy. You want your text to read as if you're having a conversation with your reader. If that means starting a sentence with **and** or **but**, that's fine. Use them. Just don't over-use them.

Over-using them at the beginning of the sentence shows your lack of knowledge of language. You should use other words to start your sentence if you begin to rely on them too much.

These are just a few basics of grammar. I can give an entire full day workshop on grammar. Hopefully these will set you on the right path.

Action: Read aloud your website text

It's a simple task today:

- Look at the main pages of your website.
- Read them aloud individually.
- Hear how they read.
- Change any grammatical mistakes you find.

Day 29 - How to Brief a Copywriter

Okay, so you've decided that you don't have the time or the motivation to write but you need the writing done. That's a good start. It acknowledges the need to continue on with your content strategy.

When you don't have the time to write yourself, there are a bunch of people out there, such as myself, who will write your message for you.

I love writing for other people; it is so much easier to write about someone else than yourself. However, the most successful projects that I have worked on are those where I had as much information as possible to begin with.

A good copy-writer will quickly understand your business and the industry you operate in. However, the key to successful copywriting is managing expectations, on both sides. You as the business-owner hiring a copy-writer must provide as much information as you can while the copy-writer must not assume to know your business.

Both parties can manage expectations when a detailed brief is written. It need not be a long document, but as long as the key information is included, you can mange expectations and create a rewarding relationship.

If your copy-writer doesn't have a brief that you can fill in, here are ten elements that I look for in a brief:

1. State the nature of your business

Simply state the nature of your business. Be as specific as you can, using your own words. For example, if you work in IT, tell me more about what it is you do, i.e. fix computers or program gaming software.

2. Describe who you want to target

Give a detailed description of your target market. Be as specific as you can, e.g.,

- Female, over 30, married or not single
- Retail units within 20 mile radius of (insert town)
- Restaurants with <50 covers

3. List your expected collateral

It is always good to know from the beginning what marketing collateral or literature you require from the project. List all the medium you require (a brochure, website, series of articles, presentation, case-study, whitepaper etc) and the amount of pages (is it a two brochure or twelve page?).

4. State your objective

So everyone is on the same page, tell the copy-writer what you want to achieve as a result of the marketing collateral. Do you want to:

- Sell a certain product
- Build credibility as an expert in the industry
- Generate leads
- Position yourself as an expert

5. Decide on a call to action

Every piece of copy that is written should have a call to action. Tell your copy-writer what it is and what you expect your reader to do after reading.

6. Know your media distribution channels

Writing on the same subject for a blog and a newspaper requires two different styles with different information contained within. Once you know which channels you're using, inform the copy-writer. Channels could include newspaper or magazine editorial, blog, video or online.

7. Share your research

This is often over-looked when briefing a copy-writer. You have information stored away on competitors, industry statistics, potential customer data. All that information that you have gathered, share with your copy-writer. Information is power once shared.

8. Decide on a tone

You have to decide on a tone for your written material. Do you want your article to be written in a tone that appears:

- educational

- chatty and informal

- conservative

- hip and trendy

- entertaining and funny

- corporate

9. Know your deadline

Sometimes copywriters need extra time to research and edit their copy. You should inform them from the get-go when they need to have the document written. This will help either side take into account the number of reviews needed so the deadline doesn't slip.

10. Have a word-count

If you're publishing an article in a paper or an advert, the newspaper or magazine only wants a required number of words. Similarly, your website might only allow a certain number of words or characters. Once you know what it is, tell your copy-writer. It will avoid unnecessary work at the end.

Once you've agreed the brief with the copy-writer, agree a budget before you start. Some people charge per article, per hour, per word. Whatever the terms, agree them in advance. That way, you will both work together to create the best possible copy which produces results.

No action today!

The only action today is to really assess whether you need the help of a copywriter. After the past 28 days, you have read and learned a great deal about writing and editing good copy.

It does take time so please take the day today to ask yourself if you've time to write elements of your content strategy. Maybe you have time to write a blog, but not four articles in a month.

Be honest with yourself – you've invested the time and money in the book so don't waste it. Consider using me to write certain elements of your strategy while you focus on the ones that you really love to write.

Just have a little think where you would like to be in 12 months and what content would you like to have out in the public domain?

If you want to use a copywriter in the end, follow the steps that I've outlined.

Day 30 - My Seven Step Writing System

Writing is definitely a task that is so easy to procrastinate on. A thousand and one things have priority over it. Sometimes writing can take so long - there is the writing, the editing, the design, the re-writing. All these tasks mean it can be put to the end of the priority or to-do list.

While writing promotional literature is creative, it can still be systematized. If you have an efficient writing system, a step by step process that you can follow, it will make it easier to sit down and write. These past 30 days have helped you with this system but today, I'm sharing with you my personal step by step process to follow when writing your next piece of literature.

Result: No more procrastination. Just great written promotional material.

Here is my seven step, **ACHIEVE Model** that I follow religiously when writing great promotional literature for clients.

Step 1: Analyze your audience

Prepare to fail or fail to prepare. This first step means taking time out to research, research, research your target audience. Who are they? Can you describe them? What do they read?

Take a detailed look at who you want to target. Find out everything you can about them - it will make it easier to target them with words and tone that they can relate to.

Step 2: Create your heading

With your research done, it's time to start on the actual literature. This is where you focus on your message(s). Central to your messages is your heading. You should build everything around your heading.

Regardless of whether it is a letter, webpage, flyer or brochure - everything should have a header. It shows your reader that you don't want to waste their time. Give them a great header and they'll read on.

Headings are not last minute items. That's where a lot of people fall down, including many of your competitors. They are the first thing you write. Remember - you can always edit it but get the basics of it down first.

Your headline or heading will make or break your promotional material. It's the gatekeeper of the article. If it's good, people will read on. If it isn't, then your email or sales letter hits the recycling bin or gets the delete button treatment.

Step 3: Handwrite your text

That's right. Take a pen and paper and start writing. Putting your fingers on the keyboard with a white page doesn't do it for many people. In my experience, it's less than 1%. If you are part of the 99% of the population, then grab a pen and paper...even if it is the back of an envelope.

When you see your hand writing and words on a page, it does something psychological to you. The creative juices start to flow. Even if it's mere words rather than actual sentences, just write them down.

Fine-tune your messages when you transfer it over to your computer. Only then, should you think about adding bullets or finessing your sentence structure.

Get all your thoughts down on paper...whatever it is that you want to say, just write it down. Don't worry about grammar, spelling or how many words you use. Use this step to tell your reader what it is you want to say - pretend they are in front of you.

Step 4 - Include your emotional triggers

Emotion plays a huge part in the buying process. You've all heard the saying "*My heart says yes but my head says no.*" What you need to do as a successful copy-writer is get inside the head of the buyer and encourage them to buy with their heart and head.

People buy from people and people buy as people. It doesn't matter if they are buying a pair of shoes, a jacket, dinner or a multi-million pound computer system. People buy to fulfill an emotional need. Thereafter, they rationalize their decisions.

You need to find out what triggers the emotions within your target market. The only way to find out is do what I talked to you about on Day 1 - Understanding your Customer. The more you find out about your customer or target market, the easier it will be to persuade them that your product or service is the right one for them

Find them and talk to those points.

Step 5: Edit your message

This is diamond step. Taking time to edit is well worth the time and money invested in doing it right. Writing is more than writing; putting words down on paper is just the start. Editing allows you to finesse your thoughts, your content, your style and tone and your spelling.

Many people confuse editing with doing a spell check. If they do a computer spell check or grammar check, then the document is edited. However, that's not the case. Editing is a process which includes a number of elements.

With all your information on paper, with your emotional hot-spots, pick and choose what is important. Start with a separate blank page and write up in short sentences your three most important points.

You know the words your readers use, you know the tone they prefer so now it's time to capture their attention and get them to read every last word you write.

Edit for style, tone, grammar, spelling, layout and actual language used.

Step 6: Vocalize your final document

Again, you've heard me right! This step is like step 3 - going back to basics. But let me ask you this - what is the purpose of your promotional material? It's to have a conversation with a prospect or a client in your absence. It takes the part of you in the conversation.

So if you want to build a rapport and engage with the reader, read your document aloud. You will soon see how it flows, how it engages or not.

This is the step where you are 100% happy with your document and feel proud to hit the publish button or send to print.

Step 7: End with a call to action

A call to action is the term to get your reader to do something after reading your letter. Every sales document that you write should have a strong call to action. This includes your sales letter, your website, your blog page, your newsletter.

Don't just think about what you want your reader to do - write it down. Every piece of promotional material should tell the reader what they need to do next. Don't write a really good headline, three captivating and compelling points and leave it hanging. Ask for something - whether it is business, that they contact you, click on an email or url. Don't assume that your reader will do anything - ask them.

Action required

This seven step process is the very one that I use every time I write something. Use it everytime you write or perhaps use it as a basis for your own writing system. It works for me so hopefully it will work for you too.

Day 31 – Take Action

Well done. Whether you followed the book on a daily basis or dipped in and out of certain chapters, by now, you will have made changes to your content and have begun relating more with your audience.

A good teacher explains what they're going to say, says it and then summarizes what they've taught.

So here it is - a summary of what you have learned over the past 150-odd pages.

Day 1 – Understanding what your Reader Wants to Read
The basic rule of copywriting – understand what your customer wants to read rather than what you want to give them.

Day 2 – What to Do if Words Don't Come Easy
Ways to research what your audience likes to read and the language they use.

Day 3 – Why Two Advil Won't Resolve Writer's Block
Treatments to avoid procrastinating.

Day 4 – How to Write Killer Headlines – The Basics

Seven basics to get right before writing a headline.

Day 5 - How to Write Killer Headlines: 4 Techniques

Four ways to write headings.

Day 6 – Another 4 Ways to Write Killer Headlines

Another four great ways to write headings.

Day 7 – The Science of Paragraph Writing

Three steps to writing a successful paragraph.

Day 8 – The Art of Paragraph Writing

How to make your paragraphs good enough to read.

Day 9 - How to Write a Successful Bulleted List

Things to consider when writing a list of bullets.

Day 10 - Getting to Grips with Sentence Structure

Tips to writing better sentences.

Day 11 - A Rough Guide to Punctuation

A list of the main punctuation marks and when to use them correctly.

Day 12 - Use Literary Devices to Make your Copy Engaging

An insight into the paintbrushes of the writing world.

Day 13 - Use Sub-Headings to Break up Your Text

Why and how sub-headings should be used in your documents.

Day 14 - Forget diamonds. Editing is the writers best friend

A checklist when editing your documents.

Day 15 - Be Careful with your Choice of Language

How to choose your words with care.

Day 16 - Writing Styles, They are a Changing

How to analyze your writing style.

Day 17 - Why you should include a P.S. Statement

Five tips when writing a P.S. Statement.

Day 18 - How to Use Call to Action in your Sales Literature

Benefits of Call to Actions and three pieces of advice.

Day 19 - The Role of Emotion in copywriting

Identifying emotional triggers and how to use them.

Day 20 - Features & Benefits - What's your Take?

The argument for leading with benefits before features.

Day 21 – Email Etiquette: The Dos and Don'ts of Emailing

Understanding email as a communication method with 7 Dos and Don'ts.

Day 22 – Writing Effective Email Subject Lines

Five Tips to Writing effective email subject lines.

Day 23 – Content is King on the Internet

Why graphics support content.

Day 24 – Measuring Copy Effectiveness

Three different ways to measure your copy, including the readability score.

Day 25 – Elements of a Content Strategy

Nine types of promotional material and the advantages and disadvantages of each.

Day 26 – 9 Steps to Writing a Successful Sales Script

Why use a sales script and nine pieces of advice.

Day 27 - The Magic Formula of copywriting

A list of motivational words proven to work.

Day 28 - A Rough Guide to Grammar

Six common mistakes in grammar and how to resolve them.

Day 29 - How to Brief a Copy-writer

Ten elements to include in your copywriter brief if you decide to hire one.

Day 30 - My Secret Writing System

Use the ACHIEVE model to write great copy.

Day 31 - Congratulations & Next Steps

Now is the time to get started. Every journey starts with the first step. You now have the tools to write great, engaging copy.

You've made the investment of both your time and money. Copywriting is the secret to good marketing. So start now writing your content marketing strategy. Time flies by so quickly so come on, make the most of your investment.

Next Steps

1. Gather your tools and start writing.

2. Edit, edit, edit

3. Publish your text – whether it's an email, a brochure to the printers, an article. Use your text. Your computer is not it's final resting place. Share it with the world.

I'm looking forward to hearing all about your journey and your results.

Email me at: 31days@achievemarketing.ie

Denise Fay

www.ingramcontent.com/pod-product-compliance
Lightning Source LLC
Chambersburg PA
CBHW051520170526
45165CB00002B/545